Ignite

98 1/2 Creative Writing Activities

DUSTY DURSTON

Published By: Novel Treasure Publishing LLC

Visit our website at www.noveltreasurepublishing.com

Edited By: Nicole d'Entremont

Cover Designed By: Miblart

Designer Website: www.miblart.com

ISBN: 978-1-951625-03-0

ACKNOWLEDGMENTS

A big thank you to my friends and family for supporting me as a writer. You continuously listen to my ideas even when they are outside the realms of reality. You watch me rollercoaster through my thoughts, self-doubt, and happy dances, with a smile and encouragement. Thank you for giving me support and letting me work through my writing process my way.

Thank you to my editor and publisher, Nicole d'Entremont, for giving me such wonderful guidance through my good times and my rookie mistakes. I've learned so much from you!

With love,

Dusty Durston

DEDICATION

This is dedicated to all who believe in the power of creativity.

OTHER BOOKS BY AUTHOR

SPARK

SPARK JR

HOW TO USE THIS BOOK

Writer's block affects everyone, from first-time writers to best-selling authors. It's one of the not-so-fun parts of the process.

And sometimes, you just need to step away from your manuscript and do something else to find inspiration.

Ignite was specifically written for just such times. The purpose of the activities in this book is to CHOP through that creative block and help you re-IGNITE your imagination.

Some creators may use one of the activities, and they are suddenly hit with the idea they needed to finish with their own project. For others, it may take more. It's different for everyone. This is a chance for you to get outside of your normal creative thought process, be outside in your surroundings, and wake up a part of your imagination that hasn't been tapped into for a while.

Because you will know all the steps in the activity upfront, be sure to not skip steps or jump ahead to the writing request. The activities were specifically designed to interact with different parts of your brain to maximize your creativity.

Don't be in such a rush that you don't get the full experience. Be honest with your answers. Getting the most out of these activities means you may have to think deeply. The more time and genuine attention you give the activity, the more you will get out of it.

If you are performing an activity and it asks you to write something down, feel free to draw it instead. Bend it to what works for you and how you want to express your end result.

These activities are grouped by where they can be most easily be completed: at home, in nature, in the classroom, or around town. It doesn't mean that you can't switch it up and do some of the at home activities in the classroom!

Work with these exercises and have fun with them. You can do any of these activities on your own or bring others in and do it as a group!

HAPPY WRITING!

ACTIVITY DISCLAIMER

Anytime you go into the wilderness, nature, etc., remember to be careful and be prepared for anything mother nature may throw at you. Let others know where you are going and when you will be back. Check-in with them if you will be late. Be safe, and take cautionary measures, so you don't get lost.

People don't like to feel stalked or on display, they don't like to have their pictures taken without their permission. Be respectful of other people's privacy. If you are going to take a picture of someone for one of the activities, get their permission first, and be honest about what you are doing.

If you start feeling a bit stalkerish, you can always use your imagination to comment on what you think this person would do, say, etc.

TABLE OF CONTENTS

1

HOME ACTIVITIES

1. Look around your house for ten random items that you can stack on top of each other. The rule is, only one of the items can touch the tabletop; the rest must build upon the others using tape, glue, or some sort of adhesive. Once it's complete, take a step back and look at your project.

If you put it on display, what would others say? Write down one comment from each of the following people: art critic, comedian, family member, friend.

2. Draw two circles that overlap from right to left (not one above the other). Keep the overlapping section of the circles empty for now.

In the circle on the far-left side, put your full name and five of your signature character traits. In the circle on the far right, write the full name of an influential person that you admire, that is not related to you, and five of their signature character traits.

Using a combination of both names create a new name and put that in the part of the circle that overlaps.

Pretend you and the influential person are both trapped in the same body, having to work together to create one answer and/or opinion to the following questions.

How would your traits blend together? Would they blend like water and oil, or would they complement each other like peanut butter and jelly?

Describe who this combined person is. What are their views on politics, religion, holidays, family, and ethics? What type of job would this person be best suited for, and what do they enjoy doing on a Friday night?

଼ଷ ଼ଡ

3. Get a friend, and each of you write the answers to five questions you've been asked before. Don't write the questions, just the answers. As a personal example, an answer I would have is… "Nope, it's just Dusty." (I always get asked if Dusty is short form something)

Read the answers to your friend and have them guess what the questions are. Then have them create a completely different

2

question where that would be the answer. An example question building upon my above answer… Is that your alien friend that just pulled up?

When you're done, review all of the questions and answers. Circle the best question and answer in your opinion and write the scene where this question took place. You must use the question and answer within the scene.

ભ્ઝ ૯૦

4. Choose a page from a coloring book. Create a legend to color-code your top 10 emotions. Every day for a month, color in sections of the picture that represent your emotions of the day. Take notes every day of the events that made or changed your emotions.

At the end of the month, write down your thoughts on any negative emotional state/responses that keep coming up. Now switch hats and become a therapist looking at your coloring page and reading your thoughts. What would they say? Why?

ભ્ઝ ૯૦

5. Close your eyes and imagine that you are rolling out of bed, full of happiness. It's your favorite season of the year, and you are reminiscing about the promotion you received a couple weeks ago. Your 1st paycheck that reflects your ginormous raise, from that promotion, hit your bank account this morning.

Think about how you would spend that money. Will you buy a new car? Will you save it for your dream house now that you can afford it? It's such a beautiful morning.

You walk out of your bedroom and into the kitchen. You pour your favorite morning drink, and it's perfect. You walk into your living room and smell something so foul, your nose shuts down.

Your life long friend is still sleeping on your couch. You asked him/her to move out 38 days ago. You agreed to let them stay for six months, and that was a year ago.

Create the dialogue between you and your friend about you looking for a new place? Do you let them move with you, stay, or is the slap of tough love coming very soon?

CB ꙮ

6. Choose five different colors of finger paint. Use one finger for each color. Put a mark on the paper and say out loud what that color reminds you of, i.e., blue may remind you of the ocean. It doesn't matter if you've never personally seen the ocean, but the blue you chose nevertheless reminds you of the ocean.

Once you're done explaining to yourself what each color reminds you of, draw a collage of those items and show those around you.

Do they know what they are? What is their reaction? It doesn't matter if you feel like the collage is good or bad, you only need to capture their facial reactions and then what their words are.

⚜ ⚜

7. Think about what scared you as a child. Now project that fear onto a creature of your own making and describe that creature.

Describe where it would live during the day and where it would live during the night. If you are lying awake in bed in a dark room, what's the first thing you would hear if it was coming towards you? Would it be footsteps? Would it be long tentacles scratching the walls?

⚜ ⚜

8. Find a picture of a zentangle. Print it out and create a legend, matching a color to each of your friends or family. For one week, every time you think of that person or talk with them color in one space of the zentangle. At the end of the week, who is the dominant person in your life, and why?

Choose the person who is least talked to and thought of and write a detailed plan on how to communicate with them more and why you want to.

If you don't want to communicate with them more explain

why. Once this is done, create a dialogue between you and this person as if they found this project and asked what was going on.

 C3   80

9. Now for a total cliché. You're stranded on a dessert island. Just joking, no island, but I really do want to talk about desserts (two S's).

Let's say you have desserts galore to choose from, and you can only choose one to eat for the rest of your life. A bit of a bummer, but any sugar is a sugar I can live with right!?

Explain in detail your top five dessert choices. What they look like, how they feel, taste, smell, etc... Why did you choose them? Would you get tired of them? Why?

C3   80

10. Choose 10 random inanimate objects. Isolate them from all other things by placing them in the corner of a room. Pile them up or put them in order however you want. They should be visible when someone enters your house.

Think about your favorite character. Write a brief description of who they are and their personality. As the objects sit in your view, describe how your favorite character would view this pile if they walked into your house and saw them.

Would they dismiss it as a clutter pile, or would they think it was the beginnings of a master plan? Would they walk over and put everything back in their proper places, ignore it, or would they kick it over to irritate you?

൬ ൭

11. Stretch! This is great, whether you're used to stretching or not. Choose any stretch you want. It can be one of your favorites or just any stretch you can remember from gym class.

Once you are in position and feeling your muscles stretch, take a few deep breathes and then imagine how that looks from the inside. Imagine the nerves sending signals to your brain.

If you could animate that conversation, what would that look like or sound like? Is it frantic yelling "STOP" or "yea, baby just like that?" What would the muscles tell you, and how? What about your bones? Your brain?

When you're done with the stretch, write down the conversation between your body parts. Give them human names but let it read as though everyone already knows the subject being spoken about.

For example, your muscle would say, "OMG, this hurts" or, "please not this again."

൬ ൭

12. Let's get into the thick of our emotions and see what overflows. Name a person in your life that you gave up on. It

could have been the right or wrong decision, it doesn't matter.

Write down what you remember. What was your perception of those last moments?

Be that other person, and what was their perception of those last moments, and why do you think they saw it that way?

೮ఇ ಜಿ

13. Take something apart. It doesn't matter if it's something electronic, wooden, or cloth. Rip the seams out of a stuffed animal, take apart that old VCR you refused to get rid of, or take apart the wooden bookshelf that's in your garage waiting to rot.

Take it apart with care noting every screw or seam or stuffed animal body part you remove. Tell a story about a character unraveling one of their treasures like you unraveling this object.

Why are they doing it? What purpose would it serve? Do they find anything inside it that shouldn't be there?

೮ఇ ಜಿ

14. Take your age and multiply it by 2, add 11, multiply by 6, add 67, multiply by your weight. Divide by 3.

Use your answer in the first blank spot in the following sentence. Use the first image that pops into your head as you're reading this to fill in the second blank spot of the sentence.

There are _____ more/less _____ in this world.

Pretend that this number is way off from normal. Explain how this number got to be so high or low.

cs so

15. Create two names that rhyme. These will be the names of a creature you've never seen before. Describe where this creature is from and what it smells like.

cs so

16. Eat vegetables! Not because your mom says so though, it's for your love of creativity. Buy five different veggies at your local store. Preferably ones you've never tried before; no cooking or seasoning it.

Create a rating system on paper or electronically for the taste, smell, and appearance. Clean it, study it, smell it, and then take a bite, and rate it.

When you're done, write about the winner and how that would make all the other veggies feel if they were alive.

cs so

17. Write this down. Little Miss Judgy Eyes. Now, what is the first thing that pops into your head? Write that down.

Continue writing down the things popping into your head for five minutes. Now write a short story about what you've written down.

CR EO

18. Make a flipbook. A flipbook is where you draw a figure on page one, and then each page after, you draw that figure in a slightly different pose, one that would suggest the figure were moving.

Once you are done, you can flip through the pages and see your character in motion. Draw your character in motion (it can be stick people) and then describe what they are doing and why.

CR EO

19. Listen to a song at random from a genre you don't like. Listen to the entire song and think about how you feel while it's being sung. Write those feelings down.

Now write down the lyrics to the song. You can google them if you don't remember all of them. Read the lyrics out loud. After you've read them aloud, what are your feelings when you read the words.

If they are different, why. If they are the same, do you have a different opinion of this genre? Why?

20. Let's test your psychic abilities. Get a deck of standard playing cards. Shuffle them thoroughly face down so you can't see them. No cheating.

Lay them in one stack face down in front of you. Get a piece of paper and make two columns. Column one is for the ones you get right. Column two is for the ones you got wrong.

Guess either the suit, number, color, or all three if you want to make it harder on yourself. Keep a tally of what you get right and what you get wrong.

Which column did you have more tally marks? Does this result predict your accuracy rate if you were to predict the future?

Let's test your theory. Write down on a piece of paper a list of things that will happen in the next thirty days and wait to see what comes true.

21. Look in the bathroom mirror. Instead of focusing on your own reflection, focus on the reflection of your surroundings.

What do the items you see, say about who you are? Let's say you woke up on the floor with amnesia. What type of person would you describe by what's in your bathroom?

22. You are going to create two different characters. Write a list of character traits for your first character.

What is their emotional state? Describe them physically. How do they react to different situations? What is their home life like? What is their friend circle or support circle like?

Create a second character the same way as you did the first, but their traits have to be the opposite of your first character.

We are now going to throw them into a few uncomfortable situations, which are listed below. You will need to create the dialogue between them for each situation.

- Office meeting where the boss is trying to decide which one to promote.

- Principal's office where the principal is asking which part each of the characters played in the senior prank that accidentally set his car on fire.

- A party where all the different cliques showed up and things are getting out of control. The party host is a mutual friend that wants everyone to leave but can't get people to listen. Both of your characters have decided to help calm things down and get people to leave.

CB ᘔ

23. High school years for most of us was not an overwhelmingly great experience, so I'll apologize upfront if I'm sending anyone back into therapy. Everyone gets labeled to some

degree in high school.

What is/was your label? Were you the cheerleader, the jock, the bully, the one who got picked on, the brain, the loner, or the class clown?

Figure out who you were and what your behavior was in the mix of things. Write down what your label was and how you got it if you know.

Do you feel like that label fit you? If yes, were you happy with it? If no, what would you have chosen to be labeled as? Do you think people's perception of you changed based on this label? Where you more than your label?

In this exercise, you and all your traits, thoughts, and feelings that you stated above are the characters.

Put yourself back in high school. Write a scene where you are surrounded by your peers, comfortable with your label, and lapping up every moment of it.

Now, in the same setting, surrounded by your peers, write a second scene where you are not okay with your label and you are trying to convince them physically or verbally, who you really are.

ᛥ ᛤ

24. Take a moment to think about how the moon pulls at the tides in the ocean. If you are unfamiliar with this, Google it and read about the effects of the gravitational pull of the tides between the Moon and the Earth.

It's quite fascinating. Ponder what it means to have something invisible be able to have such a great impact on something so far away. How can you relate that invisible pull to a character?

Your character is going to be pulled by someone or something in order for situations to happen. Create a situation that would force your character to react.

ය ෨

25. Choose five names that all start with the same letter. These are all siblings. Write a brief description of their personalities.

Once you've done this for each, put them in order of age. Now write or draw how each act with other siblings and then how they act with their parents.

ය ෨

26. Describe your sleep space. Describe what you sleep on. How does it make you feel to lay down? Are you refreshed when you wake?

Is this a good bed or an old creaky bed? Is your sleep space ideal for sleeping, or is there a mountain of laundry lying next to you ready to suffocate you in your sleep?

Using your sleep space, write a descriptive piece where you follow your character from when they begin their bedtime routine to going to sleep, then waking up.

Did they get good sleep? How does their sleep quality affect them?

❦

27. Find a YouTube channel where the person has a camera filming an activity that would scare you to death to do it yourself.

For example, somebody that is riding a dirt bike down a dangerous path or jumping off a bridge. Put the headphones on and have the picture as large as it can be. Watch that video and think about how that person is feeling.

How would you feel if you were doing that for the first time? Would you be able to take that first step? What drives somebody to do potentially dangerous activities? What do you think the adrenaline rush feels like to them and then compare it to what it would feel like for you?

❦

28. Meditate every morning for seven days. Start with two minutes and add one minute each day, so on day seven, you will meditate for eight minutes. If you are unsure how to meditate, get help from a meditation coach that can guide you through this process.

Prior to this meditation exercise, research why meditation is used.

What do you think? Was it what you thought it would be?

Will you continue or not? Draw or describe a character that uses meditation as a superpower.

☙ ❧

29. Find pictures of different patents. You can do this online through the United States Patent and Trademark Office. Search for something that speaks to you.

Study the picture and what it's supposed to be used for. Write a description to explain it being used for a completely different reason.

☙ ❧

30. Take an emotional intelligence test. You can find one online. Create four characters that have different variations of your emotional intelligence, you being one of those characters.

Write the dialogue between you and them where you are trying to get out of a difficult situation.

☙ ❧

31. Create three outfits that suit you but represent three very different personalities. Have a friend take multiple pictures of you wearing each of these outfits. Review them. Have fun with the posing and be true to character.

How would these personalities fit together in a story?

ᛣ ᛤ

32. Let's say you're being followed by the paparazzi. You can be as truthful or fake as you want for this exercise. Explain why you're being followed.

What would the paparazzi take pictures of on your best day? What would they take pictures of on your worst day?

ᛣ ᛤ

33. What's a T.V. show that you absolutely hate? Why? Create a character that you would have liked to have seen in the show. If you added them, how would this change the dynamic of the show?

ᛣ ᛤ

34. Purchase a newspaper or magazine that is notorious for having outlandish stories that are often untrue. Read through the entire magazine. Choose five stories that you think may be true or mostly true.

Why do you believe them over the others?

Choose one out of the five stories and write the sequel to it. No holds barred, go for it.

35. Choose your favorite social media platform and find the person you like the best. Describe why. Are their posts vibrant, dark in nature, cute and cuddly?

Choose a handful of pictures/posts that you like from that person and try to recreate them.

Are yours better or worse? Why? If this other person saw your posts, what do you think they would say based on the personality you see on their social media page?

CR BD

36. Take an apple and eat half of it. Write down how it tastes, looks, and smells. Now place the uneaten half on a plate or somewhere it can't be touched.

Imagine this fruit has feelings and is a person. Every three days, note what it looks like, how you think it would taste (actually tasting it is at your own risk), describe the smell and write down how this apple feels.

Do this for the next 15 days.

CR BD

37. Let's bedazzle something. Gather up some craft gems, glue, and a coloring page.. Now, bedazzle the heck out of your coloring page. Fill that page up!

Now go show your friends your great artwork. Look and act

genuine when talking about how amazing it looks and you're thinking of selling it. Watch their faces and note their responses.

If you are naturally a good artist and make spectacular bedazzled items, then try to do a not so good job. You're trying to get people's reactions.

38. Choose two religions that seem to be opposite in theology. Research how each one was created and why it was created. Describe a faithful follower of each. Create the dialogue between the two regarding one of their opposing views.

39. Choose an object that is small enough to put in your pocket but is not an everyday object. Buy one if you need to. Now pretend this is your lucky item. Explain in writing or in a picture why it is lucky. Create the story behind it?

40. Create a nursery rhyme that is no more than ten lines long. There has to be a moral to the rhyme. Why did you choose that moral?

41. Let's say you got a flat tire and found yourself on the side of the road. It's desolate and there are no cars in sight. As you're sitting there, a tow truck pulls up, and the person inside asked if you need a tow.

What are your thoughts? What do you do?

If you decide to get in the tow truck, explain the conversation that you would have with the tow person.

What does he or she look like? Why did they become a tow truck driver?

What happens if you open the glove box and find a gun? How does that change your original thought of that person?

CB ED

42. Lay in the dark. It doesn't matter what time it is, but it does have to be dark. As close to pitch black as possible. There needs to be minimal noise.

Softly count to 10 and listen to your voice. Concentrate and linger on each letter/word enunciated.

How does it sound? What character would you create with that voice?

Explain why they are whispering, counting from 1-10?

Now count to ten with your voice at a normal volume, and then again with a loud volume.

Each time create a different character for that voice and answer the question of why.

43. Choose your favorite type of weather. Create a world where that is the only weather there is. It never changes. Write down or draw the pros and cons.

How would you feel mentally, physically, and spiritually if it was always that weather? How would it affect recreation, food source, relationships, jobs, etc.?

44. Choose a drink you don't like like coffee, tea, wine, or beer. Taste test five different varieties of that drink. Rate them and create a character personality for each based on the taste. If choosing alcohol, be safe, and drink responsibly.

45. Make a video of something out of character for you. It has to include all the senses. Sight, sound, taste, touch, smell, and intuition. Watch it and critique your work.

46. As you are blindfolded have a friend hand you soft, non-harmful objects that are coated in something that isn't normal for that object.

For example, you may be handed a pencil covered in peanut butter or a piece of paper that is soaking wet. The objects chosen by your friend need to remain a secret, you can't know.

As you hold them, try and identify the objects. How do they feel? How did you feel when holding these objects? Is it hard to concentrate on the object because of what it is covered in?

❧ ❧

47. Try to mimic sounds that animals make. Use at least five different animals. Is it difficult? Which one is the most difficult, and why? How do you feel unleashing these sounds?

❧ ❧

48. Invent a game. Send it to a toy company. Every week write down your thoughts on what your chances are of it getting accepted. Do this for eight weeks or until you receive a response.

How do you feel about the response? If you don't receive a response, write how you feel about that?

❧ ❧

49. Our sense of smell can be very powerful when it comes to

jogging our memory or adjusting our attitude; good or bad. Let's test this out.

Create a one-month calendar. Every day, make a note describing your mood? This can be one word if you want.

Next to your , write down if you were aware of any smells and how that affected you.

What were your favorite smells each month? Do you find that your mood and the smells correlate?

50. Look through a photo album or something like a yearbook you have memories from. Reminisce about one particular event that is dear to you.

Ladies, you cannot choose the birth of your child for this exercise. Now remove yourself from the equation.

How would it be different for you and everyone there? Were you the main guest?

If so, what would be the reason you didn't make it. Create the event where you were instead and describe why you chose that event over the one from your memory.

2

AROUND TOWN ACTIVITIES

51. Go to a coffee shop and order a drink you've never tried before. Before you take the first sip, smell your drink, and write down what you smell.

Is it good or bad? What do you think of when you smell it? Describe what you are anticipating this drink to taste like. Now taste the drink. Describe if it's how you imagined it or not.

If it's not, describe how it tastes and how/why it's different than what you thought. Write two different sets of dialogue between you and someone you know as if they were drinking it with you for the first time.

One dialogue should be your coffee drinking partner agreeing with you, and the other dialogue should show how they disagree with you.

ಿ ಜ

52. Go to a cemetery you haven't been to before and walk around. Read the headstones that call to you or that just look interesting. Pretend to be a family member that has come to visit.

Read the words out loud on the headstone in the voice of that family member. If you must wait for others to walk out of earshot, that's fine.

Once you have identified the family member and their voice, have a one-sided conversation confessing something that you (as the family member) did to the deceased. Play it up and go into detail about the predicament, what happened, how it happened, and why it happened.

Is that predicament what landed them in that grave? Go into detail as to why you are now confessing.

Once this is done, write down the conversation you just had and the details of the family member you were pretending to be. If you are compelled to continue this story, please do so.

ಿ ಜ

53. Put a stain of something on your shirt and, for the entire day, watch peoples' reactions to that stain.

Create a log of people that noticed your stain, noting who

they are if known, physical description, and what they said about it, or if they didn't say anything at all.

Next, write what you believe their character profile would be based on your observation.

 beginenumerate
CB   BD

54. Choose an animal that you have never touched before and go spend some time with it. For example, I had never petted a pig before and I was very surprised at how it felt.

A little caution, do not pet wild animals, try the petting zoo, pet store, or a friends' pet. Always ask permission from the owner to pet their animal.

Write down how you felt when you first approached this animal. Were you nervous, excited, scared?

Write a poem of the animal without naming it. Take your poem to your friends or social media and ask if someone can guess which animal you are talking about.

CB   BD

55. Go to your local museum and watch the people going in and out from the parking lot or front entrance. Choose the person you find particularly interesting and write down their description and what a conversation would be like with them based on your observations.

Once that is done, go into the museum and find the display you think this person would be most attracted to. Write down your reason why.

CB ꙮ

56. Go to the zoo and people watch. Look at the individuals and match them to the animals in the zoo. Why would you pair them up? Is it their looks, their demeanor, something they said?

Create the dialogue between you and a police officer where you are describing each person using the animals as comparisons so that they can create a character sketch.

CB ꙮ

57. Take a video recording device with you. Drive to a rural area and find a crossroads that is not well-traveled. If you cannot get to this point, use your imagination and think about a crossroads you've seen before.

Pull off to the side of the road where it's safe. Get out of the car if you are comfortable doing so. Stand off to the side of the road, never in the middle. No need to get hit by a car.

Start recording your surroundings, and as you record, speak out loud what your surroundings are. Look around, what do you see? Stand for a minute or so looking in each direction, North, East, South, West.

Are there any differences in the landscape? What do you

smell? If someone has passed you by, what kind of look are they giving you? Did they stop and ask if you need help?

After you have talked about everything you see, go home and watch your video. Now that you are in the comfort of your own home, what would you have said differently?

Write the dialogue between two people that are stranded at that same location.

抗 抖

58. Attend a class that teaches something you've never done before. Go with friends, family, or by yourself. Note how you are feeling in the hours before class starts. Take a mental note of how you feel as you walk into the class.

What does it smell like? Who are the others in the class? Write this all down as you go. If you can't, then do it after the class is over. Write down how you feel afterward. Accomplished? Drained? Angry? Happy?

Now draw or write a character having a conversation with a friend expressing what you just went through.

抗 抖

59. Go to a mall or a shopping area that is known to draw in a more financially established crowd. People watch. Just sit and write what you see, hear, and smell.

If you decide to get a bite to eat while there, what are your choices, and how did it taste? Now go to a mall or shopping area that attracts working-class folks who are on a tight budget. Do the same.

Once you have that finished, picture a big line drawn in the sand, and you have a handful of both groups of people standing at that line facing each other. Ask them to converse.

Create those conversations in your mind or write them down. Remember not to fall into the cliché or stereotypes in these groups. Looks can deceive, and people can surprise you.

Will one of your character surprise someone standing on the other side of that line?

CȜ ȣ

60. Choose your favorite color. Go take 10 pictures of something or someone that has that color as the dominant color on them. Each picture has to be from a different angle. Look at these pictures and describe what they have in common, and you can't use any color at all.

CȜ ȣ

61. Draw a tic tac toe board but have six squares across and six squares down. Color each square a different color, including the end squares that may not have the line on the end.

Go out into the world and write down what you see that has

that color on it. Write it on top of the color square. Once that is complete, go to your creative space and write about or draw all of these things fitting together.

Not necessarily how they fit together physically, but are they similar? Can they be used together? Do they go together? Now create a story with them.

CB BO

62. When doing this exercise, think about a domino effect. When you go to the store, take a mental note or write down who is around you. Note the tiny amount of interaction you have with them. Think about how these interactions make you feel.

We all sense things when we look at others. Some people get angry just by looking at someone because they dress or talk a certain way.

Maybe you see an elderly lady, and your heart goes out to them because they remind you of your wonderful grandmother. Pay attention to how people in the store make you feel even though you don't interact with them.

When you get home, sit down and pretend that on your way to that same store and you end up in a minor fender bender. You exchanged insurance cards with the person; no real damage was done, but you know at some point you'll be dealing with insurance agents, time off work, etc. Because of this, agitation has set in as you walk into the store.

Now, let's say you run into the same people as before. How would your agitated state change your perception and your initial emotional reaction to them?

⚜ ⚜

63. Take a long-distance train trip. Go by yourself or go with friends or family. Look out the window and daydream about what's going on out there.

Spend the time imagining another world where you'd be in a better situation than what you are now and with new friends and a different family.

Create conversations between you and your new friends and family about who you were before you switched to your new life.

⚜ ⚜

64. Time for some foot action, and I'm not talking about a pedicure. I'm talking about going outside and taking a walk.

Take your camera or if your phone has a camera that will work too. I want you to take pictures of five different objects or animals. You are going to create a new world using these five objects.

Print out the pictures. They can be printed on regular paper stock if you don't have photo paper, but make sure they are in color.

31

On a poster board size paper, tape or glue the pictures you took. These objects or animals have now become the symbol for each location on the map. One object or animal will represent one location.

Draw landscape around the objects that represents the city/ town/community of that location. Write why these objects/ animals are the symbols for the location.

For example, if you take a picture of water, maybe they use water magic. Maybe they are abundant with water and at the source, so they determine how much will flow into each river. Each area has its own type of social status.

Describe how these work within each location and how they interact with their neighboring locations.

ೞ ೲ

65. Go to a department store that sells all kinds of things from garden items to clothes to toys to food. Walk around straightening the shelves or racks.

Note if you are getting strange looks, and if people are starting to ask you where things are, or if you're asked to stop.

While straightening these items, how does it feel to do so? Does it feel overwhelming to think about doing this for an entire row?

Does it give you satisfaction to have things tidied up? Are you getting frustrated that people are messing things up after you just straightened up?

❦ ❧

66. Next time you're out around people, be sure to say hi to everyone that gets within 10 feet of you. Write down their responses and write down what you think they are saying in their head based on the look and response they give you.

❦ ❧

67. Go to an assisted living home and talk with some of the residents. Ask them what their family is like. Ask them what school was like, what their grandparents were like, really get in-depth with who they were, and where they are now.

Looking back, are they happy with how things turned out, or what would they have changed?

❦ ❧

68. Choose five stores that you have never been in before. Humans are creatures of habit, so the stores we wind up going to the most are the stores that we are attracted to and are comfortable with.

While you're in the stores, find one item from each store that you like and wouldn't normally find in your regular stores. Buy each of those items and take them home with you.

If you can't buy them, then take a picture of them. Explain why you like them.

69. Sit on the outer edge of a parking lot that is fairly busy. Watch people as they drive in, park, and communicate with each other.

Choose a family or a person that you are drawn to, and explain why they're there. Explain what their childhood was like and how they ended up at this location on this day.

3

NATURE ACTIVITIES

70. Nature time! Wherever you can find nature, go to it. This could be the mountains, a section of trees, the plains, or your garden. Remember what I said earlier about being careful.

If you go out past your garden, make sure to be safe and let others know where you are going. Take a chair with you and sit in nature for a while. Don't think about your home life, work, or even trying to chop this creative block.

Soak in your surroundings. Think about what you see. If you see plants, vegetation, trees, think about how they get nutrients.

How do they grow, how does the water and nutrients from the ground climb up that plant and circulate throughout the entire plant?

If you could see the nutrients flowing through the plant or tree, what would that look like? Is it a circular motion, clockwise, counterclockwise? Does it go straight up and stop at the top?

It doesn't matter if you know the correct answer or not, this is what your imagination is creating. Visualize that process as if you can see it happening in real-time, then write it down or draw it as if you are explaining it to someone else.

ᘓ ᘔ

71. Go outside! Go out and just listen. Get comfortable in an outdoor space and close your eyes (if it's safe) and listen to what is going on around you.

What do you hear? Is it out of place or what you anticipated? Take what you hear and mentally place that sound in an odd setting at an odd time of the day or night.

For example, if you hear the clanking of a garbage can lid, imagine that noise in a zero-waste community at one in the morning and write down why you would be hearing it there and at that time.

ᘓ ᘔ

72. Get dirty! Grab some potting soil or just some dirt from your yard and run your hands in and out of it.

How does that feel? Is it getting under your nails? Is that

good or bad? What does the soil look like? Light, dark, sandy? Do you rub the dirt off with a towel or wash your hands? Why?

What would your character do if they were forced to do this? Would they love it? Would they refuse? Why?

❧ ☙

73. Find a flower or plant that really draws you in. Write down or draw its description. Now go online and google only the descriptive words.

What do you get? How are the two similar. How are they different?

❧ ☙

74. Catch a bug. Make sure the little thing has enough air but is secure. We don't want to harm it. Once you've caught it, watch and study it.

Describe how it's moving around. Now create the inner dialogue it's having. Put it back where you found it.

❧ ☙

75. Time for some sun. After you put on some sunscreen because safety is key. Lay in the sun and have your front or your back facing the sun while the other side is not touched by

the sun. Close your eyes and observe how your body feels on one side versus the other.

Are the sun's hot rays beating down heavily on one side with a coolness on the other side? How does this feeling and your observations play into your characters or drawings?

You may have two characters in the same situation that are having two separate experiences. Write or draw two separate people in the same setting but having opposite or different experiences.

76. Go to a lake or slow running stream. Somewhere, quiet. Pick a rock about the size of your fist. Quietly watch everything around you as you hold the rock in your hand. What sounds do you hear?

After a few minutes throw the rock into the water and listen to the sound it makes. Sit and replay that sound in your head. Now imagine you're camping next to a body of water all alone and you hear that noise.

What conclusions would your brain jump to within that first few seconds? After the initial thought, your brain will begin to rationalize the noise. How would your brain rationalize that noise?

77. Find some treasure in nature! It doesn't have to be good treasure, but anything you can find value in. Go walking in the forest, the countryside, or the plains.

As you are walking, look down and find things that grabs your interest or calls to you. It could be a pretty rock, a bottle cap, or an arrowhead. The possibilities are endless.

When you find something of interest, take it home and explain in writing or in a picture how it got there.

4

CLASSROOM ACTIVITIES

78. Create ten columns and five rows on a piece of paper. In the first row, write one word in each box going across that describes your favorite movie or book. In the second row, write ten words, one in each box going across that describes your favorite season.

Follow this same format to describe your favorite food, music, and game (board, card, video). You will end up with ten words across and five words down.

Roll dice or toss a coin onto your columns. Whichever column it lands on is the column of words you must use.

Write a four-sentence paragraph about anything you want, but you must use all five of those words.

Explain to someone what type of story this paragraph

would fit in and why. Do they agree? If not, why?

⋆ ⋆

79. Have a friend create or buy five items. They can't tell you what they are (no sharp or potentially harmful objects). As you are blindfolded, touch the objects at length and speak out loud, the characteristics of what you're touching.

Once you have described the objects by just touching them, guess what they are and talk about how could they be used in a story.

⋆ ⋆

80. Group time – ten-player game. Feel free to modify this if you are not in a group. Cut 30 squares of paper 1 in x 1 in. Separate them into three equal piles of ten.

- Pile one: Write ten different emotions, one on each square.

- Pile two: write ten different countries, one on each square.

- Pile three: write ten different numbers between 17-80, one on each square.

Everyone will pull one square from each category. You will use these squares to describe a character.

The emotion will represent your character's typical emotional state on most days, the country is their birth country, and the number represents their age.

Write a couple of paragraphs about that character.

Next, everyone will read out loud who their character is. As a group, everyone must decide how these characters fit together. Are they lifelong friends, part of a club, or maybe they are meeting each other for the first time?

ೞ ෨

81. Choose a board game that you enjoy playing. Call your friend(s) over and read the list of rules that came with the game. You and your friends can create entirely new rules as you go.

Pretend you're all four-year-olds that don't like to lose. Observe the dynamics of your group and how the new rules affect the game as a whole.

How does it affect the other players individually? Write down your observations.

ೞ ෨

82. Wear gloves all day; the thicker, the better. What type of looks did you get from others? Did you get a lot of questions? What was your response? How was it to not feel the world

around you?

If your character were to be lost emotionally to where they refused to have feelings anymore, compare your inability to feel with your hands to their inability to feel with their emotions.

ɠ ɞ

83. Create 11 sentences that form a story. Write it down. Each sentence has to have the word left or right in it at least one time. Have a group of friends sit in a circle and have one person hold an object.

As you read the story, the participants have to pass the object to their left or right as you say the word. Whoever ends up with that object has to tell a story about themselves and how they know you.

After your friends leave, write a story about the ones who didn't say a story. If they all told a story, write about the friend whose story surprised you the most.

ɠ ɞ

84. Nothing will get you to be more creative than when you're running away from numbers. Just kidding mathletes!

On a piece of paper, write the numbers 1 – 10 going down the paper. Assign each number a color and write that color next to your number.

Your challenge is to create a piece of art using the colors and the number of times of that color.

Example, if purple equals five, then whatever you create has to have five purples sections or pieces on it. When you're finished, explain your creation.

ભ ટ

85. Dive into a research project. Choose a different culture or era from what you know. Perform an internet search and see what you find. Put yourself in that era with your current personality, thoughts, and opinions.

How would you feel, act, and react to what was going on in around you? Would you fit in or would you be considered an outcast?

ભ ટ

86. Spend time with someone you don't know very well. Be safe and smart about this meeting. Don't meet with a complete stranger, always meet in a public place, and let other people know who you will be meeting.

Get to know them by asking them questions. Create the questions in advance and perform an interview.

Once your questions are answered, write or draw a short story about them. The story can be fiction or non-fiction.

൙ ൠ

87. Find or buy a puzzle that is somewhat difficult to put together. Put that puzzle together by yourself. Note your feelings before, during, and after that puzzle is completed.

Now find another puzzle with the same amount of difficulty. Find one or more friends and put that puzzle together in one sitting if possible.

Describe your feelings before, during, and after this experience. How do the two experiences compare? What did you like better, and why?

൙ ൠ

88. For 30 days, write one note per day to someone. Make it something positive. Don't warn them ahead of time. Just give it to them. Write down any responses you get.

൙ ൠ

89. Use the opposite hand for the day. How did it make you feel? Did your perspective on anything change?

൙ ൠ

90. Join a group that piques your curiosity. If you are usually an introvert, then join a group that pulls you out of

your comfort zone. If you are an extrovert, join a group that relishes in quiet, solitary activities that they do alongside each other.

At the end of the session or multiple sessions, ask them questions about why they prefer this group over something that you would normally choose to be a part of.

What are the responses? And why?

☙ ❧

91. Create a message, lecture, or teaching that you would hear from an astrology teacher or an ancient history teacher. This can be truth or fiction. Create as much detail as you can on how it affects the culture today.

☙ ❧

92. Go to YouTube and find a children's channel that does challenges. There are things like the 3 am challenge, food challenges, bubble wrap challenges, etc. Try three challenges that seem fun to you.

Once you have completed the challenges, choose which one you liked best, and create instructions for others that want to perform this challenge.

The instructions should include how to prepare for the challenge and include a list of items needed. You will explain how best to win the challenge and any helpful tips.

Have your friends do it with you and create a review section at the end of your instructions. This can be written or in video format.

93. Paint blindfolded. Have a friend guide you through the process of making a simple painting. They will hand you the paintbrush and change the paint colors as needed.

You won't know what color you are painting with. Follow their instructions on how to paint.

You will do two different paintings. One time while they are softly speaking the directions. The second time they will give the same directions in an abrupt and angry manner.

Note the difference in paintings and how were you feeling as you painted each of them.

94. Write a book review on a story that you read only because of the cover. Be honest in your review. Take note of why you were attracted to the cover and do you think the cover matched the book.

95. Toss a ball around with a friend or bounce it off something if you're by yourself. Each time you get the ball, make a fictional statement.

It can be something you've read or entirely of your own creation. You have to be quick because you can only hold the ball for five seconds before you have to throw it again.

Do this at least ten times.

How hard was it for you to say these statements within the five seconds? Were there times you couldn't get something out before having to throw the ball again? What statement did you like the best and why?

※　※

96. Pay attention to your inner thoughts as you are listening to other people's conversations. In your mind, replay those internal thoughts using a voice that is not your own.

For example, you can use a ghoulish voice, a heavy breather voice, or a snobby voice, etc. Make it fun. Try creating a few different voices.

As you are replaying other people's conversations in your head using different voices, what types of characters are popping into your mind?

Write down what these characters look like. When you've written down all your characters, put them in a room together, and create a dialogue between them.

97. On your dominant hand, tape your pointer and middle fingers together. Go through your entire day like that.

What were the difficulties? What kind of looks did you get from people? What questions were you asked, and how did you respond?

98. For one week, wear the same color shirt. If you choose blue, it can be variations of blue, but it still has to be blue.

How does this change your routine? Have your thoughts changed? How? Did people say anything?

If so, what? How many people actually noticed? What is your relationship with those that noticed and those that did not?

98 ½. Pretend someone comes to you asking for help to chop through their creative block. Create an activity to help them.

ABOUT THE AUTHOR

Dusty is someone who loves to write. Like all of you readers and writers out there, she loves spending time with her imagination on a regular basis. She hopes that all of her readers will have fun with her books.

CONNECT WITH THE AUTHOR

Website: www.DustyDurston.com

Facebook: https://www.facebook.com/DustyDurston/

Instagram: https://www.instagram.com/dusty_durston/

Pinterest: https://www.pinterest.com/DustyEDurston/

Bookbub: https://www.bookbub.com/profile/dusty-durston?list=about

Made in the USA
Columbia, SC
28 February 2022